Find Out About...
Britain Since 1930

48 Differentiated Key Stage 2 Non-Fiction Texts with Questions

Introduction

Find Out About Britain Since 1930 is a collection of twelve different topics explored at four different reading levels. It is aimed at the busy teacher who needs to accurately differentiate classroom work to make sure all pupils in their care are working towards their maximum potential. The Levels used match the English National Curriculum. The Level 2 texts have a passage to copy out with missing words to be found. The remaining texts have simple factual questions in Section A and more open-ended/ inferred questions in Section B. Section C suggest ideas for illustrating the work. All the pages have been printed 'Landscape' to make maximum use of the space on Interactive Whiteboards. Black and white images are used in the paper book; full colour images have been used in the e.book and download.

Topical Resources publishes a range of Educational Materials for use in Primary Schools and Pre-School Nurseries and Playgroups.

For the latest catalogue:
Tel 01772 863158
Fax 01772 866153
email: sales@topical-resources.co.uk
Visit our Website at:
www.topical-resources.co.uk

Copyright © Peter Bell
First Published April 2011
ISBN 978-1-907269-55-4

Illustrated by John Hutchinson, Art Works, Fairhaven, 69 Worden Lane, Leyland, Preston

Designed by Paul Sealey, PS3 Creative, 3 Wentworth Drive, Thornton, Lancashire

Printed in the UK for 'Topical Resources' by T. Snape and Co Ltd., Boltons Court, Preston, Lancashire

Contents

1. Kings and Queens of Britain 1930 - 2010
   - Level 2 2
   - Level 3 3
   - Level 4 4
   - Level 5 5

2. Britain in the 1930s
   - Level 2 6
   - Level 3 7
   - Level 4 8
   - Level 5 9

3. World War II
   - Level 2 10
   - Level 3 11
   - Level 4 12
   - Level 5 13

4. Memories of an Evacuee
   - Level 2 14
   - Level 3 15
   - Level 4 16
   - Level 5 17

5. The Home Front
   - Level 2 18
   - Level 3 19
   - Level 4 20
   - Level 5 21

6. Changes in Shopping 1930 - 2010
   - Level 2 22
   - Level 3 23
   - Level 4 24
   - Level 5 25

7. Changes in the Home 1930 - 2010
   - Level 2 26
   - Level 3 27
   - Level 4 28
   - Level 5 29

8. The Rise of 'Pop Music'
   - Level 2 30
   - Level 3 31
   - Level 4 32
   - Level 5 33

9. Travel by Car
   - Level 2 34
   - Level 3 35
   - Level 4 36
   - Level 5 37

10. Passenger Aircraft and Holidays Abroad
    - Level 2 38
    - Level 3 39
    - Level 4 40
    - Level 5 41

11. Early Space Travel
    - Level 2 . . . . . . .4:
    - Level 3 . . . . . . .4:
    - Level 4 . . . . . . .4.
    - Level 5 . . . . . . .4!

12. The Computer Age
    - Level 2 46
    - Level 3 47
    - Level 4 48
    - Level 5 49

Kings and Queens of Britain 1930 - 2010

King George V became King in 1910. He was the grandson of Queen Victoria. He changed his German family name to Windsor in 1917. King Edward VIII became King in 1936. He chose to give up the throne so he could marry a divorced American lady. King George VI was Edward's brother. He had not expected to become King. He found it very difficult to give important speeches.

Queen Elizabeth II became Queen in 1952. She was crowned in 1953 at Westminster Abbey. She has four children, Charles, Anne, Andrew and Edward.

George V   Edward VIII   George VI   Elizabeth II

Copy this writing and fill in the gaps:

Kings and Queens of Britain 1930 - 2010

In _____ King George V became King. He was Queen Victoria's _____. In 1917 he changed his German family name to_____. In _____ King Edward VIII became King. He chose to give up the throne so he could marry a divorced _____ lady. King George VI was Edward's_____. He found it very difficult to give _____ speeches. In 1952 Queen Elizabeth II became Queen. She was crowned in 1953 at _____Abbey. She has four children, Charles, _____, Andrew and Edward.

Kings and Queens of Britain 1930 - 2010

King George V became King of Britain in 1910. He was the grandson of Queen Victoria and Prince Albert. He changed his German family name to Windsor in 1917 after the First World War.

King Edward VIII became King in 1936. Only months after he became King he caused a national crisis by proposing to marry Wallis Simpson, an American who had already been married twice before. Edward chose to abdicate (give up the throne).

King George VI was Edward's brother. He also became King in 1936. King George had not expected to become King and was reluctant to do so because he had a stammer. This meant that he found it very difficult to give important speeches.

Queen Elizabeth II became Queen in 1952 when her father died. She was crowned Queen in 1953 at a grand ceremony held at Westminster Abbey. She has four children, Charles, Anne, Andrew and Edward. She has lived longer than any previous British King or Queen.

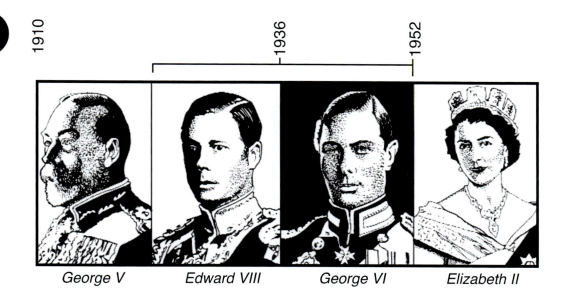

George V *Edward VIII* *George VI* *Elizabeth II*

Answer these questions:

Section A
1. When did George V become King of Britain?
2. Who was George V's grandmother?
3. When did Edward VIII become King of Britain?
4. What relation was George VI to Edward VIII?
5. Why did George VI not want to become king?
6. When did Elizabeth II become Queen?
7. What are Elizabeth II's children called?

Section B
1. Why do you think King George V changed his name?
2. What does it mean for a King to abdicate?

Section C
Carefully draw a timeline of British Kings and Queens from 1930.

Kings and Queens of Britain 1930 - 2010

King George V was King of Britain from 1910 until his death in 1936. He was the grandson of Queen Victoria and her German husband, Prince Albert. George V reigned throughout the First World War when the British fought against Germany. Because of anti-German public opinion he changed his German family name to Windsor in 1917.

King Edward VIII became King in 1936. Only months after he became King he caused a national crisis by proposing to marry Wallis Simpson, an American who had already been married twice before. Rather than give up Mrs Simpson, Edward chose to abdicate (give up the throne).

King George VI was Edward's brother. He became King in 1936 after Edward abdicated. George VI had not expected to become King and was reluctant to do so because he had a stammer. This meant that he found it very difficult to give a speech during important occasions.

Queen Elizabeth II became Queen in 1952 when her father died. She was crowned Queen in 1953 at a grand ceremony held at Westminster Abbey which was seen for the first time by people throughout the country on black and white televisions. She has four children, Charles, Anne, Andrew and Edward. She has lived longer than any previous British King or Queen.

1910   1936   1952

George V   *Edward VIII*   *George VI*   *Elizabeth II*

Answer these questions:

Section A
1 When did George V become King of Britain?
2 Who was George V's grandmother?
3 When did Edward VIII become King of Britain?
4 What relation was George VI to Edward VIII?
5 Why did George VI not want to become King?
6 When did Elizabeth II become Queen?
7 What are Elizabeth's children called?
8 What is unique about Queen Elizabeth II?

Section B
1 Why do you think King George V changed his name?
2 What does it mean for a King to abdicate?
3 Why did King George not expect to become King?
4 Why was Elizabeth's coronation seen by more people than ever before?

Section C
Carefully draw a timeline of British Kings and Queens from 1930.

© Topical Resources. May be photocopied for classroom use only.

Kings and Queens of Britain 1930 - 2010

Kings and Queens are the names given to male and female rulers of countries. Kings and Queens once ruled in many parts of the world and had real power in their lands. They passed on this power through the family line. Today, in Britain, the Queen's role is largely ceremonial. This means the government of the day runs the country while the Queen supports their work by presiding over special occasions.

King George V was King of the United Kingdom, the British Dominions and the Emperor of India from 1910 until his death in 1936. He was the grandson of Queen Victoria and her German husband, Prince Albert of Saxe-Coburg and Gotha. George V reigned throughout the First World War when the British fought against Germany. Because of anti-German public opinion he changed his German family name to Windsor in 1917. He died in 1936 after a long illness.

King Edward VIII became King in 1936. Only months after he became King he caused a national crisis by proposing to marry Wallis Simpson, an American who had already been married twice before. For political and religious reasons the government would not allow the marriage to go ahead. Rather than give up Mrs Simpson, Edward chose to abdicate (give up the throne). With a reign of only 325 days, Edward was one of the shortest reigning British Kings. He was never crowned.

King George VI was Edward's brother. He became King in 1936 after Edward abdicated. King George had not expected to become King and was reluctant to do so because he had a stammer. This meant that he found it very difficult to give a speech during important occasions. However, with the help of a speech specialist, Lionel Logue, he overcame this difficulty and was able to make many encouraging speeches during the Second World War. He had two daughters, Elizabeth and Margaret.

Queen Elizabeth II became Queen in 1952 when her father died. She was crowned Queen in 1953 at a grand ceremony held at Westminster Abbey which was seen for the first time by people throughout the country on black and white televisions. She has four children, Charles, Anne, Andrew and Edward. She has lived longer than any previous British King or Queen and at the time of writing continues as Queen of England and Head of the Commonwealth of Nations.

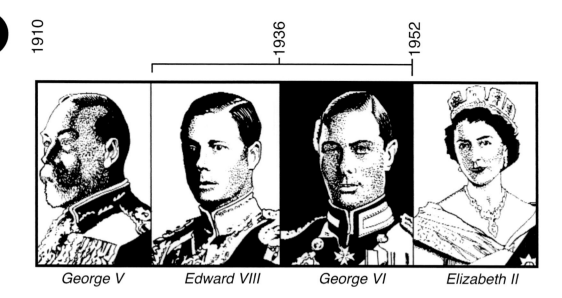

George V   *Edward VIII*   *George VI*   *Elizabeth II*

Answer these questions:

Section A
1. When did George V become King of Britain?
2. Who was George V's grandmother?
3. When did Edward VIII become King of Britain?
4. What relation was George VI to Edward VIII?
5. Why did George VI not want to become King?
6. When did Elizabeth II become Queen?
7. What are Elizabeth's children called?
8. What is unique about Queen Elizabeth II?
9. What is a King or a Queen?

Section B
1. Why do you think King George V changed his name?
2. What does it mean for a King to abdicate?
3. Why did King George V not expect to become King?
4. Why was Elizabeth's coronation seen by more people than ever before?
5. What is the role of the Queen in Britain today?
6. How do you think Edward VIII felt about abdicating?
7. How do you think George VI felt when he became King?

Section C
Carefully draw a timeline of British Kings and Queens from 1930.

Britain in the 1930s

Most goods such as clothes, shoes and pottery found in British homes were made in Britain. In the 1930s many British people lost jobs because other countries started making things. People who lost their jobs applied for 'dole' money to help them buy food. In 1936 a town called Jarrow had so many people out of work they organised a walk to London to complain. Not everyone was out of work. During the 1930s many old houses were knocked down and new ones built.

Copy this writing and fill in the gaps:

Britain in the 1930s

Most goods such as _____, shoes and clothes found in British homes were made in Britain. Many British people lost _____ in the 1930s because other countries started making things. To help them buy ____ people who lost their jobs applied for 'dole' money. A town called _____ had so many people out of work they organised a walk to London to complain in 1936. Not everyone was out of _____. Many old _____ were knocked down and new ones built during the 1930s.

Level 2

© Topical Resources. May be photocopied for classroom use only.

Britain in the 1930s

Before the 1930s most goods such as clothes, shoes and pottery found in British homes were made in Britain. Many British people lost their jobs because other countries started making things and selling them in Britain cheaply.

People out of work applied for the 'dole', government money to help them survive. A man from the dole office would inspect a home and order people to sell things such as pictures or a piano before they were given any help.

In 1936 a town called Jarrow had so many people out of work they organised a march to London as a protest. Two hundred marchers travelled from Jarrow to London. When they arrived they were given the train fare home but very little changed in their town.

Not everyone was out of work. During the 1930s many of the old Victorian terraced houses were knocked down and new ones built. The greatest improvement in the new homes was the use of electricity.

Answer these questions:

Section A
1. Where were most household goods made before the 1930s?
2. Why did many British people lose their jobs?
3. How did people out of work survive?
4. Which town organised a march to London?
5. How many marchers made the journey to London?
6. Which houses were replaced during the 1930s?
7. What was the greatest improvement in the new homes?

Section B
1. What do you think about other countries making and selling things?
2. How would you feel about the dole office inspecting your home for things you may be ordered to sell?

Section C
Carefully draw and colour the Jarrow march.

Britain in the 1930s

Before the 1930s most goods such as clothes, shoes, pottery and machines found in British homes were made in Britain. Some parts of Britain were famous for making ships, but in the 1930s nobody wanted new ships. Many cotton workers lost their jobs because people in India, Japan and China were making their own cotton into clothes and selling them more cheaply.

People out of work and with no savings applied for the 'dole', government money to help them survive. A man from the dole office would inspect a home and order people to sell possessions such as ornaments, pictures or a piano before they were given any help.

In 1936 a town in the north called Jarrow had so many people out of work they organised a march to London as a protest. Two hundred marchers travelled from Jarrow to the Palace of Westminster, a distance of almost 300 miles. When they arrived in London they were given the train fare home but very little changed in their town.

Not everyone was out of work. During the 1930s many of the old Victorian terraced houses were knocked down and new ones built. The greatest improvement in the new homes was the use of electricity. In 1922 there were only 2 million homes with electricity, by 1939 there were 11 million.

Answer these questions:

Section A
1 Where were most household goods made before the 1930s?
2 Why did many British people lose their jobs?
3 How did people out of work survive?
4 Which town organised a march to London?
5 How many marchers made the journey to London?
6 Which houses were replaced during the 1930s?
7 What was the greatest improvement in the new homes?
8 Which countries started making cotton into clothes?

Section B
1 What do you think about other countries making and selling things?
2 How would you feel about the dole office inspecting your home for things you may be ordered to sell?
3 What made the people of Jarrow march to London?
4 How do you think the people felt after the march?

Section C
Carefully draw and colour the Jarrow march.

Level 4 — © **Topical Resources.** May be photocopied for classroom use only. — page 8

Britain in the 1930s

Before the 1930s most goods such as clothes, shoes, pottery and machines found in British homes were made in Britain. These goods were also sold to other countries providing plenty of work. During the 1930s people in other countries could no longer afford to buy British goods. Instead they made things themselves, often more cheaply. This resulted in a slump in British factories.

Some parts of Britain were famous for making ships, but in the 1930s nobody wanted new ships. The shipyards could not pay the wages for the men and so they were put out of work. Many cotton workers lost their jobs because people in India, Japan and China were making their own cotton into clothes and selling them more cheaply. Britain had many coalmines to provide coal to heat people's houses and run the steam-powered railways. When factories were closed, fewer goods travelled by train, less coal was needed and so many coal miners lost their jobs. Living in Britain became very difficult because there had never been as many people with no job.

People out of work and with no savings applied for the 'dole', government money to help them survive. A man from the dole office would inspect a home and order people to sell possessions such as ornaments, pictures or a piano before they were given any help. This upset many people who had saved hard for these things.

In 1936 a town in the north called Jarrow had so many people out of work they organised a march to London to protest. Two hundred marchers travelled from Jarrow to the Palace of Westminster, a distance of almost 300 miles. The men were led by a mouth organ band and supported by a bus carrying cooking equipment. As they passed through towns, local people would give up some of their own food to help support the men. When they arrived in London they were given the train fare home but very little changed in their town.

Not everyone was out of work. During the 1930s many of the old Victorian terraced houses were knocked down and new ones built providing work for bricklayers and carpenters. Many private homes were built as well as new council estates. The greatest improvement in the new homes was the use of electricity. In 1922 there were only 2 million homes with electricity, by 1939 there were 11 million. The cinema was very popular for entertainment with towns having many different ones to choose from. The radio became popular in the home.

Answer these questions:

Section A
1. Where were most household goods made before the 1930s?
2. Why did many British people lose their jobs?
3. How did people out of work survive?
4. Which town organised a march to London?
5. How many marchers made the journey to London?
6. Which houses were replaced during the 1930s?
7. What was the greatest improvement in the new homes?
8. Which countries started making cotton into clothes?
9. What new work became available in the 1930s?

Section B
1. What do you think about other countries making and selling things?
2. How would you feel about the dole office inspecting your home for things you may be ordered to sell?
3. What made the people of Jarrow march to London?
4. How do you think the people felt after the march?
5. Why did many coal miners lose their jobs?
6. What do you think people thought about using electricity for the first time?
7. Why do you think cinemas were so popular during the 1930s?

Section C
Carefully draw and colour the Jarrow march.

World War II

World War II started when Germany invaded Poland in 1939. Britain and France declared war on Germany. Eventually, Germany, Italy and Japan were at war with Britain, France, Russia and the United States. The war was fought on land, sea and in the air. People suffered from the bombing. On land, there were tank battles. At sea, submarines sank ships. During the war many cities and towns were badly damaged. It took many years for countries to be rebuilt.

Copy this writing and fill in the gaps:

World War II

When Germany invaded _____ in 1939 World War II started. France and _____ declared war on Germany. Eventually, Germany, ____ and Italy were at war with Britain, France, the United States and ____. The war was fought on land, ___ and in the air. People suffered from the _____. Tank _____ took place on the land. Submarines sank _____ at sea. During the war many cities and towns were badly _____. It took many years for countries to be rebuilt.

World War II

World War II started when Germany invaded Poland in 1939. Britain and France declared war on Germany. Eventually, Germany, Italy and Japan (the Axis powers) were at war with Britain, France, Russia, the United States and other nations (the Allies). The war was fought on land, sea and in the air.

MAIN EVENTS

June 1940 – German forces capture France.
Sept. 1940 – Bombing raids start in Britain.
June 1941 – Germany invades Russia.
Dec. 1941 – Japanese attack Pearl Harbour.
Oct. 1942 – Germans and Italians defeated in Africa.
June 1944 – Allies invade Normandy, France.
Jan. 1945 – Russians invade Germany from the east.
March 1945 – Allies enter Germany from the west.
May 1945 –The war in Europe ends.
Aug. 1945 – Japan surrenders.

During this terrible war many cities and towns were badly damaged and food was scarce. It took many years for countries to be rebuilt.

Answer these questions:

Section A
1. When did World War II start?
2. Which countries belonged to the 'Axis Powers'?
3. Which countries belonged to the 'Allies'?
4. Where was the war fought?
5. When did the Germans capture France?
6. When was Britain bombed?
7. When did the Japanese attack Pearl Harbour?

Section B
1. Why do you think this was described as a 'terrible war'?
2. Why do you think it took a long time for countries to be rebuilt?

Section C
Carefully draw and colour a picture of a bombing raid.

World War II

World War II started when Germany invaded Poland in 1939. Britain and France declared war on Germany. Eventually, Germany, Italy and Japan (the Axis powers) were at war with Britain, France, Russia, the United States and other nations (the Allies). The war was fought on land, sea and in the air. New inventions such as radar and rocket propelled missiles were used for the first time.

MAIN EVENTS

Sept. 1939 – Germany invades Poland. Britain and France declare war on Germany.

June 1940 – German forces capture France.

Summer 1940 – RAF defends the English Channel.

Sept. 1940 – Bombing raids start in Britain.

June 1941 – Germany invades Russia.

Dec. 1941 – Japanese attack Pearl Harbour.

Oct. 1942 – Allies defeat Germans and Italians in Africa.

Sept. 1943 – Italy surrenders.

June 1944 – Allies invade Normandy, France.

Jan. 1945 – Russians invade Germany from the east.

March 1945 – Allies enter Germany from the west.

May 1945 –The war in Europe ends.

Aug. 1945 – Japan surrenders and World War II ends.

During this terrible war many cities and towns were badly damaged and food was scarce. It took many years for countries to be rebuilt and past hatreds forgotten.

Answer these questions:

Section A
1 When did World War II start?
2 Which countries belonged to the 'Axis Powers'?
3 Which countries belonged to the 'Allies'?
4 Where was the war fought?
5 When did the Germans capture France?
6 When was Britain bombed?
7 When did the Japanese attack Pearl Harbour?
8 When did Italy surrender?

Section B
1 Why do you think this was described as a 'terrible war'?
2 Why do you think it took a long time for countries to be rebuilt?
3 Why do you think new inventions were used in this war?
4 What does the phrase 'past hatreds forgotten' mean?

Section C
Carefully draw and colour a picture of a bombing raid.

World War II

World War II started when Germany invaded Poland in 1939. Britain and France declared war on Germany. Eventually, Germany, Italy and Japan (the Axis powers) were at war with Britain, France, Russia, the United States and other nations (the Allies). The war was fought on land, sea and in the air. Civilians suffered from the bombing of towns and cities. On land, there were huge tank battles in Russia and North Africa. At sea, submarines sank many cargo ships. New inventions such as radar and rocket propelled missiles were used for the first time.

MAIN EVENTS
Sept. 1939 – Germany invades Poland. Britain and France declare war on Germany.
April 1940 – German forces capture Norway and much of Western Europe.
June 1940 – German forces capture France.
Summer 1940 – RAF defends the English Channel during the Battle of Britain.
Sept. 1940 – Bombing raids start in Britain.
June 1941 – Germany invades Russia.
Dec. 1941 – Japanese attack Pearl Harbour, a deep water American Naval base, bringing the Americans into the war.
Feb. 1942 – Japanese capture Singapore.
May 1942 – American Navy defeats Japanese in the Battle of the Coral Sea.
June 1942 – Allies invade North Africa.
Oct. 1942 – Allies defeat Germans and Italians in North Africa.
Nov. 1942 – Russians defeat Germans at Stalingrad.
July 1943 – Allies land in Southern Italy.
Sept. 1943 – Italy surrenders.
June 1944 – Allies invade Normandy, France.
July 1944 – Plot to kill Adolf Hitler fails.
Oct. 1944 – US fleet defeats the Japanese in the biggest naval battle of the war.
Jan. 1945 – Russians invade Germany from the east.
March 1945 – Allies enter Germany from the west.
April 1945 – Hitler commits suicide in Berlin. The war in Europe ends in May.
Aug. 1945 – Americans drop atomic bombs on Hiroshima and Nagasaki. Japan surrenders and World War II ends.

During this terrible war many cities and towns were badly damaged and food was scarce. It took many years for countries to be rebuilt and past hatreds forgotten.

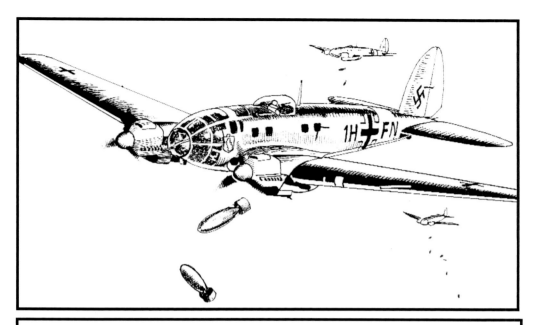

Answer these questions:

Section A
1. When did World War II start?
2. Which countries belonged to the 'Axis Powers'?
3. Which countries belonged to the 'Allies'?
4. Where was the war fought?
5. When did the Germans capture France?
6. When was Britain bombed?
7. When did the Japanese attack Pearl Harbour?
8. When did Italy surrender?
9. When did the war end in Europe?

Section B
1. Why do you think this was described as a 'terrible war'?
2. Why do you think it took a long time for countries to be repaired?
3. Why do you think new inventions were used in this war?
4. What does the phrase 'past hatreds forgotten' mean?
5. What is a civilian?
6. Why do you think Adolf Hitler committed suicide?
7. Why do you think Japan surrendered?

Section C
Carefully draw and colour a picture of a bombing raid.

Memories of an Evacuee

"Our teacher told us we were to be evacuated.

We had to carry our gas masks and a small case

with our clothes. When we arrived the local nurse

immediately checked our hair for nits! We were

sent to live on a farm with two other boy

evacuees. It was quite different from home. There

was no running water and no electricity.

I remember people were very kind to us. Our

teacher set up a classroom in the hall of the local

school. I was there for three years."

Copy this writing and fill in the gaps:

Memories of an Evacuee

"Our teacher told us we were to be _____. We had to carry a small case with our _____ and our gas masks. The local _____ checked our hair for nits immediately we arrived! We were sent to live on a _____ with two other boy evacuees. It was quite different from home. There was no _____ and no running water. I remember people were very kind to us. Our teacher set up a _____ in the hall of the local school. I was there for three years."

Level 2   © Topical Resources. May be photocopied for classroom use only.   page 14

Memories of an Evacuee

"Our teacher told us we were to be evacuated. We had to carry our gas masks and a small case with our clothes. When we arrived the local nurse immediately checked our hair for nits!

We were sent to live on a farm with two other boy evacuees. It was quite different from home. There was no running water and no electricity. I remember people were very kind to us.

Our teacher set up a classroom in the hall of the local school. I was there for three years. One Easter, we went home to Belfast. The German planes came over and a firebomb landed in our upstairs bedroom. I didn't sleep at all that night.

When I was 14 I had to return to Belfast to start work. My dad found me a job as a sheet metal worker. I helped to make ships for the war effort. They were very difficult times."

Answer these questions:

Section A
1. Who told the children they were to be evacuated?
2. What did the children have to take with them?
3. Where were the children sent to live?
4. How was this different from home?
5. How were the children treated?
6. Where did the children go to school?
7. Why did the child speaking have to return home?

Section B
1. How do you think most children would have felt when they were told they would be evacuated?
2. How do you think the speaker felt when a bomb landed in the upstairs bedroom?

Section C
Carefully draw and colour a picture of a child being evacuated.

Memories of an Evacuee

"When our teacher informed us we were to be evacuated we were quite excited by the news. We had to carry our gas masks and a small case with our clothes. When we arrived the local nurse immediately checked our hair for nits!

We were sent to live on a farm with two other boy evacuees. It was quite different from home. There was no running water so we had to get washed outside by the well. The farmhouse had no electricity so we were sent to the town for paraffin to run the oil lamps. I remember people were very kind to us.

Our teacher set up a classroom in the hall of the local school. I was there for three years. One Easter, we went home to Belfast. The German planes came over and we had to hide under the stairs. A firebomb landed in our upstairs bedroom and I heard men running up the stairs to throw it out of the window. I didn't sleep at all that night.

When I was 14 I had to return to Belfast to start work. My dad found me a job as an apprentice sheet metal worker. I made long metal heating ducts which were used in the ships that were being built for the war effort. They were very difficult times."

Answer these questions:

Section A
1. Who told the children they were to be evacuated?
2. What did the children have to take with them?
3. Where were the children sent to live?
4. How was this different from home?
5. How were the children treated?
6. Where did the children go to school?
7. Why did the child speaking have to return home when he was 14?
8. What did he do when he returned to Belfast?

Section B
1. How do you think most children would have felt when they were told they would be evacuated?
2. How do you think the speaker felt when a bomb landed in the upstairs bedroom?
3. Do you think the speaker would have liked living on the farm?
4. Why do you think the speaker went home 'one Easter'?

Section C
Carefully draw and colour a picture of a child being evacuated.

Level 4   © Topical Resources. May be photocopied for classroom use only.

Memories of an Evacuee

George Stewart was 11 years old when war was declared on 3rd September 1939. Here are some of his memories of those times:

"I lived in Belfast with my Dad and two brothers. Our mother died when I was just seven. My Dad thought at first his boys should be evacuated to Canada to avoid the bombing of the shipyards in Belfast. However, he changed his mind on September 4th when he heard that a German Submarine called the U-30 had sunk the Athenia, a ship carrying over 1000 passengers to Canada. Instead we were evacuated to Warrenpoint.

When our teacher informed us we were to be evacuated we were quite excited by the news, although some children really did not want to leave home. Our class teacher took us 70 miles into the country by bus and by train. We had to carry our gas masks and a small case with our clothes. When we arrived the local nurse immediately checked our hair for nits!

We were sent to live on a farm with two other boy evacuees. It was quite different from home. There was no running water so we had to get washed outside by the well. The farmhouse had no electricity so we were sent to the town for paraffin to run the oil lamps. I remember people were very kind to us. The farm had five dogs as well as herds of cows and flocks of sheep. After school we would help out with jobs such as picking potatoes or gathering hay. I remember once being trapped against a wall by a cow with long horns. I reached up to the ceiling beams and dragged myself up to escape!

Our teacher from Belfast set up a classroom in the hall of the local school. I was there for three years. Our father came to visit us from time to time. One Easter, we went home to Belfast. The German planes came over and we had to hide under the stairs. A firebomb landed in our upstairs bedroom and I heard men running up the stairs to throw it out of the window. I didn't sleep at all that night. When I got back to the farm the next day I just flopped on the bed and slept.

When I was 14 I had to return to Belfast to start work. My dad found me a job as an apprentice sheet metal worker. I had no say in the matter; it was just what I had to do. I made long metal heating ducts which were used in the ships that were being built for the war effort. They were very difficult times."

Answer these questions:

Section A
1. Who told the children they were to be evacuated?
2. What did the children have to take with them?
3. Where were the children sent to live?
4. How was this different from home?
5. How were the children treated?
6. Where did the children go to school?
7. Why did the child speaking have to return home when he was 14?
8. What did he do when he returned to Belfast?
9. What sort of jobs did the children do on the farm?

Section B
1. How do you think most children would have felt when they were told they would be evacuated?
2. How do you think the speaker felt when a bomb landed in the upstairs bedroom?
3. Do you think the speaker would have liked living on the farm?
4. Why do you think the speaker went home 'one Easter'?
5. Why was the speaker not sent to Canada?
6. Where was the speaker sent instead of Canada?
7. How do you think the speaker felt after escaping from the cow?

Section C
Carefully draw and colour a picture of a child being evacuated.

The Home Front

World War II was the first war in which ordinary people were in danger. To stop enemy aircraft finding cities during the night, every house was ordered to put up heavy black curtains. To keep people safe during bombing raids the government encouraged the use of air raid shelters. The government appealed for volunteers to defend Britain's coastline. At first they had to make do with borrowed weapons. Later they were properly equipped and became known as the Home Guard.

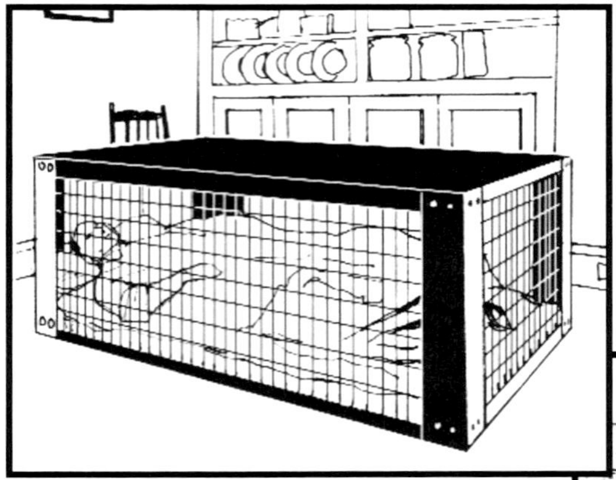

Morrison Shelter

Anderson Shelter

Copy this writing and fill in the gaps:

The Home Front

World War II was the first _____ in which ordinary people were in danger. Every house was ordered to put up heavy black _____ to stop enemy aircraft finding cities during the night. The government encouraged the use of air raid _____ to keep people safe during bombing raids. To defend Britain's _____ the government appealed for volunteers. At first they had to make do with _____ weapons. Later they were properly equipped and became known as the _____ Guard.

Level 2

© Topical Resources. May be photocopied for classroom use only.

page 18

The Home Front

World War II was the first war in which ordinary people were in danger. The first German bombing raid took place over London in September 1940.

In an attempt to stop enemy aircraft finding cities during the night, streetlights were turned off and every house was ordered to put up blackout curtains. Heavy black curtains were used to make sure light did not appear through any windows.

To keep people safe during bombing raids the government encouraged the use of air raid shelters. People with gardens could build an Anderson shelter made of corrugated sheets of steel bolted together. Morrison Shelters looked like a heavy-duty steel table with mesh around the sides.

In 1940 the government made an urgent appeal on the radio for volunteers to defend Britain's coastline. At first they had to make do with borrowed weapons. Later they were properly equipped and became known as the Home Guard.

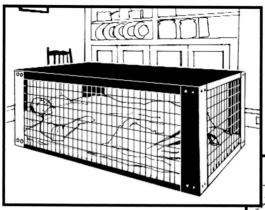
Anderson Shelter

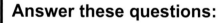
Morrison Shelter

Answer these questions:

Section A
1. When did the first German bombing raid take place?
2. Why were the streetlights turned off?
3. What were the heavy black curtains used for?
4. Why were air raid shelters used?
5. What was an Anderson shelter made from?
6. What did a Morrison shelter look like?
7. Why did the government appeal for volunteers?

Section B
1. What do you think it would be like walking about in a town at night with no streetlights?
2. What do you think it would be like to sleep in an air raid shelter?

Section C
Carefully draw and colour a picture of an air raid shelter.

The Home Front

World War II was the first war in which ordinary people were in danger from enemy troops. The first German bombing raid took place over London in September 1940. Within months Liverpool, Birmingham, Coventry and other cities were hit.

In an attempt to stop enemy aircraft finding cities during the night, streetlights were turned off and every house was ordered to put up blackout curtains. Heavy black curtains were used to make sure even tiny gaps of light did not appear through any windows. Blackout wardens patrolled the streets and fined people if their curtains were not shut.

To keep people safe during bombing raids the government encouraged the use of air raid shelters. People with gardens could build an Anderson shelter. This was made of corrugated sheets of steel bolted together. Morrison Shelters looked like a heavy-duty steel table with mesh around the sides. People sleeping in these were protected from falling debris but could become trapped if the house collapsed.

In May 1940 the government made an urgent appeal on the radio for volunteers to defend Britain's coastline. Within 24 hours 250,000 men had volunteered for the Local Defence Volunteers. At first they had to make do with borrowed shotguns, pistols and home made weapons. Later they were properly equipped and became known as the Home Guard.

Morrison Shelter

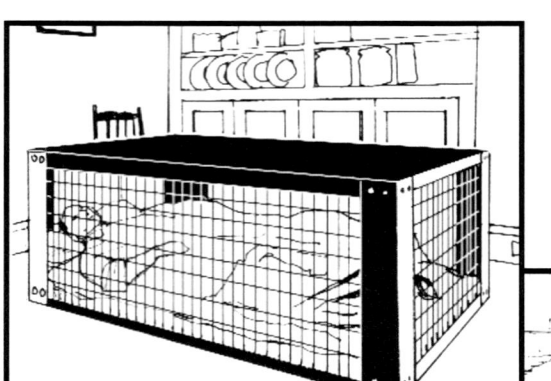

Anderson Shelter

Answer these questions:

Section A
1 When did the first German bombing raid take place?
2 Why were the streetlights turned off?
3 What were the heavy black curtains used for?
4 Why were air raid shelters used?
5 What was an Anderson shelter made from?
6 What did a Morrison shelter look like?
7 Why did the government appeal for volunteers?
8 What did the volunteers become known as?

Section B
1 What do you think it would be like walking about in a town at night with no streetlights?
2 What do you think it would be like to sleep in an air raid shelter?
3 Why do you think this was the first war in which ordinary people were in danger?
4 Why do you think so many people quickly volunteered for the Local Defence Volunteers?

Section C
Carefully draw and colour a picture of an air raid shelter.

Level 4

The Home Front

World War II was the first war in which civilians were in danger from enemy troops. The first German bombing raid took place over London in September 1940. Within months Liverpool, Birmingham, Coventry and other cities were hit. The government issued everyone with gas masks in case the Germans decided to use gas bombs. Gas masks had to be taken everywhere you went.

In an attempt to stop enemy aircraft finding cities during the night, streetlights were turned off and every house was ordered to put up blackout curtains. Heavy black curtains were used to make sure even tiny gaps of light did not appear through any windows. Blackout wardens patrolled the streets and fined people if their curtains were not shut or had any gaps in them. Cars and lorries had shutters fitted to their headlamps so only a tiny beam of light appeared from them which could not be seen from above.

To keep people safe during bombing raids the government encouraged the use of air raid shelters. In London people slept in Underground stations. People with gardens could build an Anderson shelter. This was made of corrugated sheets of steel bolted together. This was half sunk into the ground and then covered with earth. People didn't like sleeping in these shelters, as they were cold, damp and liable to flooding in heavy rain. Morrison Shelters looked like a heavy-duty steel table with mesh around the sides. People sleeping in these were protected from falling debris but could become trapped if the house collapsed.

In May 1940 the Government made an urgent appeal on the radio for volunteers to defend the 5000 miles of Britain's coastline. They were concerned that German paratroopers may be dropped into the country while most of the army was fighting in Europe. They appealed to all men aged between 17 and 65 who were not serving in the armed forces. Within 24 hours 250,000 men had volunteered for the Local Defence Volunteers. At first they had to make do with borrowed shotguns, pistols and home made weapons. Later they were properly equipped and became known as the Home Guard.

Before the war, much of Britain's food was imported by ship. Owing to the threat to shipping posed by submarines the government launched the 'Dig for Victory' campaign. People were urged to use gardens and every spare piece of land such as parks, tennis courts and golf courses to grow vegetables.

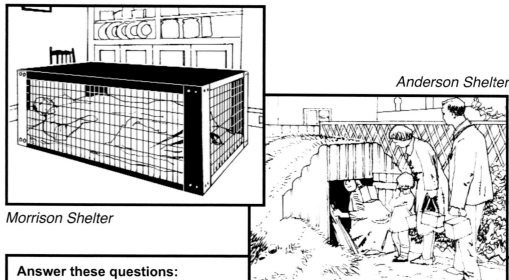

Anderson Shelter

Morrison Shelter

Answer these questions:

Section A
1. When did the first German bombing raid take place?
2. Why were the streetlights turned off?
3. What were the heavy black curtains used for?
4. Why were air raid shelters used?
5. What was an Anderson shelter made from?
6. What did a Morrison shelter look like?
7. Why did the government appeal for volunteers?
8. What did the volunteers become known as?
9. How did people 'Dig for Victory'?

Section B
1. What do you think it would be like walking about in a town at night with no streetlights?
2. What do you think it would be like to sleep in an air raid shelter?
3. Why do you think this was the first war in which civilians were in danger?
4. Why do you think so many people volunteered for the Local Defence Volunteers?
5. What does 'imported by ship' mean?
6. What was the threat posed by submarines?
7. What do you think it would be like to wear a gas mask?

Section C
Carefully draw and colour a picture of an air raid shelter.

Changes in Shopping 1930 - 2010

In the 1930s most homes did not have a fridge.

The milkman delivered milk early each morning.

Fruit was grown locally and only available when

ripe. During World War II there was not enough of

every type of food to go round and so some foods

had to be rationed. During the 1950s and 1960s

most people shopped daily in a high street.

People would queue up and wait to be served.

During the 1970s people served themselves in

supermarkets, which contained all types of food.

Copy this writing and fill in the gaps:

Changes in Shopping 1930 - 2010

Most homes did not have a _____ in the 1930s. Early each morning the _____ delivered milk. Fruit was only available when _____ and grown locally. During World War II there was not enough of every type of food to go round and so some foods had to be _____. During the 1950s and 1960s most people _____ daily in a high street. People would _____ up and wait to be served. During the 1970s people served themselves in _____, which contained all types of food.

Level 2   © Topical Resources. May be photocopied for classroom use only.   page 22

Changes in Shopping 1930 - 2010

In the 1930s most homes did not have a fridge. Instead, they had a larder or a pantry. Milk could not be kept longer than a day so a milkman delivered it early each morning. Fruit was grown locally and only available when ripe.

During World War II there was not enough of every type of food to go round and so some foods had to be rationed. A typical ration for one person for one week may include 110g of butter, 340g of sugar, 110g of bacon and 2 eggs.

During the 1950s and 1960s most people shopped daily in a high street with separate dairy, butchers, fishmongers, green grocers, ironmongers and clothes shops. People would queue up and wait to be served.

During the 1970s supermarkets became popular. They were large stores containing all types of food where you served yourself. The use of fridges and freezers meant that food could now be stored for much longer periods of time.

Answer these questions:

Section A
1. What did most homes have instead of a fridge?
2. Why did the milkman deliver milk every day?
3. When was fruit available?
4. When were foods first rationed?
5. Where did most people shop during the 50s and 60s?
6. Why did people queue up in shops?
7. When did supermarkets become popular?

Section B
1. Why do you think people in the 1950s and 1960s went shopping every day?
2. What difference do you think owning a fridge and a freezer made to doing your shopping?

Section C
Carefully draw and colour a picture of a lady shopping.

Changes in Shopping 1930 - 2010

In the 1930s most homes did not have a fridge. Instead, they had a larder or a pantry. Milk could not be kept longer than a day so a milkman delivered it early each morning. Fruit was seasonal. For example, strawberries were not available in the winter; they were only available when they could be grown fresh and within a short travelling distance.

During World War II there was not enough of every type of food to go round and so some foods had to be rationed. Ration Books were given out containing tokens, which entitled each person to buy certain foods. A typical ration for one person for one week may include 110g of butter, 340g of sugar, 110g of bacon and 2 eggs.

During the 1950s and 1960s most people shopped daily in a high street with separate dairy, butchers, fishmongers, green grocers, ironmongers and clothes shops. People would queue up and wait to be served. They would describe or point out what they wanted and it would be fetched, weighed and wrapped up for them often while having a conversation with the sales assistant.

During the 1970s supermarkets became popular. They were large stores containing all types of food where you served yourself. The use of fridges and freezers meant that food could now be stored for much longer periods of time.

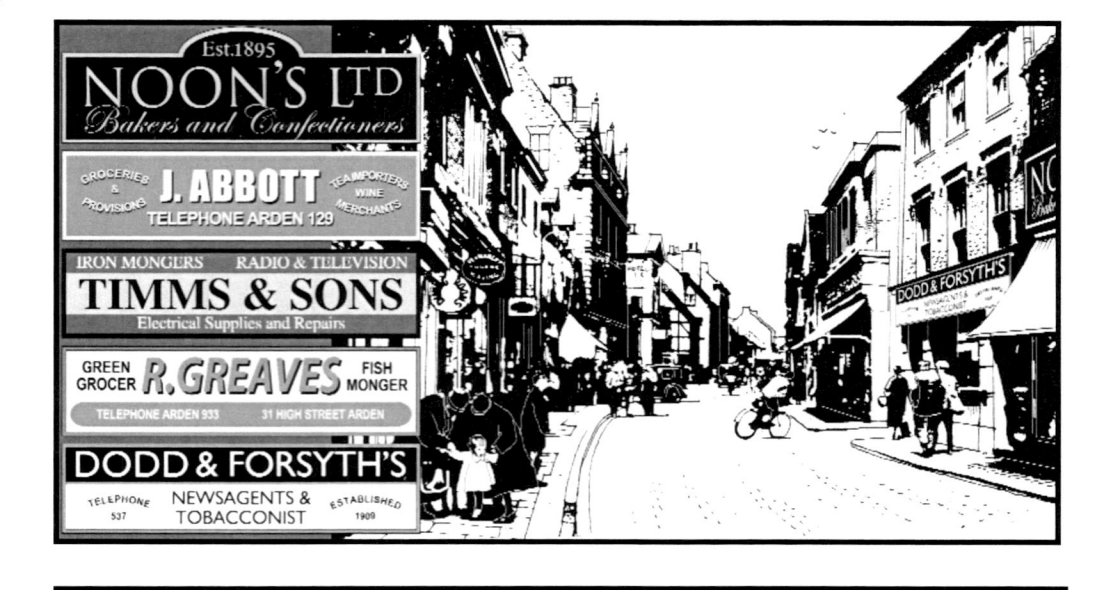

Answer these questions:

Section A
1 What did most homes have instead of a fridge?
2 Why did the milkman deliver milk every day?
3 When was fruit available?
4 When were foods first rationed?
5 Where did most people shop during the 50s and 60s?
6 Why did people queue up in shops?
7 When did supermarkets become popular?
8 Describe a typical ration for one person for one week.

Section B
1 Why do you think people in the 1950s and 1960s went shopping every day?
2 What difference do you think owning a fridge and a freezer made to doing your shopping?
3 Why would shopping in the 1950s take longer than shopping today?
4 Why was shopping in the 1950s more sociable than shopping now?

Section C
Carefully draw and colour a picture of a lady shopping.

Changes in Shopping 1930 - 2010

In the 1930s most homes did not have a fridge. Instead, they had a larder or a pantry. This was a small, well-ventilated brick built room in which to keep food fresh. Milk could not be kept longer than a day so a milkman delivered it early each morning. Fruit was seasonal. For example, strawberries were not available in the winter. They were only available when they could be grown fresh within a short travelling distance. Bananas and oranges were brought in by ship. During World War II they were not available at all because it was so difficult to have them delivered.

During World War II, there was not enough of every type of food to go round and so some foods had to be rationed. Ration Books were given out containing tokens, which entitled each person to buy certain foods. A typical ration for one person for one week may include 110g of butter, 340g of sugar, 110g of bacon and 2 eggs. People were encouraged to plant vegetables in their gardens to make the food go further. Food rationing continued until 1953.

Clothes were also rationed. This affected women more than men because they couldn't get silk stockings. Some women did all sorts of things to make it look as if they were wearing stockings such as staining their legs with tea and drawing a line to represent a seam. Jackets and jumpers were patched at the elbow to make them last as long as possible.

During the 1950s and 1960s most people shopped daily in a high street with separate dairy, butchers, fishmongers, green grocers, ironmongers and clothes shops. People would queue up and wait to be served. They would generally describe or point out what they wanted and it would be fetched, weighed and wrapped up for them often while having a conversation with the sales assistant.

During the 1970s supermarkets became popular. They were large stores containing all types of food where you served yourself. As people became wealthier they purchased cars to drive to the supermarket and do all of their shopping for a week, or even a month, rather than shopping daily. The use of fridges and freezers meant that food could now be stored for much longer periods of time. Recently, shopping on the Internet has become popular. People log on to their favourite supermarket, draw up a list of foods they require and the store delivers to the door.

Answer these questions:

Section A
1. What did most homes have instead of a fridge?
2. Why did the milkman deliver milk every day?
3. When was fruit available?
4. When were foods first rationed?
5. Where did most people shop during the 50s and 60s?
6. Why did people queue up in shops?
7. When did supermarkets become popular?
8. Describe a typical ration for one person for one week.
9. What type of shopping has recently become popular?

Section B
1. Why do you think people in the 1950s and 1960s went shopping every day?
2. What difference do you think owning a fridge and a freezer made to doing your shopping?
3. Why would shopping in the 1950s take longer than shopping today?
4. Why was shopping in the 1950s more sociable than shopping now?
5. Why do you think it was difficult to have bananas delivered during the war?
6. Why do you think clothes rationing affected women more than men?
7. Why do you think Internet shopping has become popular?

Section C
Carefully draw and colour a picture of a lady shopping.

Changes in the Home 1930 - 2010

In the 1930s the main source of heating was the coal fire. People listened to the wireless. In the 1950s gas fires heated many homes and the first televisions began to appear. The radiogram played records. By the 1970s many homes were heated with central heating and colour televisions became popular. In the 1990s freezers and tumble driers were popular. Computers started to become common. In the 2010s computers are connected to the Internet. Large flat screen TVs are connected to hundreds of channels. People chat or text on mobile phones.

Copy this writing and fill in the gaps:

Changes in the Home 1930 - 2010

The main source of heating was the coal _____ in the 1930s. People listened to the _____. Gas fires heated many homes and the first _____ began to appear in the 1950s. The radiogram played records. By the 1970s many homes were heated with _____ heating and colour televisions became popular. In the 1990s tumble driers and _____ were popular. Computers started to become common. In the 2010s computers are connected to the _____. Large flat screen TVs are connected to hundreds of _____. People chat or text on _____ phones.

Level 2 © Topical Resources. May be photocopied for classroom use only. page 26

Changes in the Home 1930 - 2010

In the 1930s the main source of heating was the coal fire. Kitchen sinks only had cold water taps. People listened to the wireless and the gramophone.

In the 1950s gas fires heated many homes and sinks now had a hot tap. The first black and white televisions began to appear. The radiogram played records.

By the 1970s many homes were heated with central heating. Kitchens now had fridges. Colour televisions became popular along with Hi-Fi systems playing records and tapes.

In the 1990s freezers, tumble driers and microwave ovens became popular. Music systems were much smaller and played CDs. Computers and computer games started to become common.

In the 2010s computers are connected to the Internet. Large flat screen TVs on the wall are connected to hundreds of channels. People chat or text on mobile phones.

Answer these questions:

Section A
1. How were houses heated in the 1930s?
2. How were people entertained in the 1930s?
3. When did black and white televisions become popular?
4. How were homes heated in the 1970s?
5. How would you play a tape in the 1970s?
6. When did computers become common?
7. What do people use mobile phones for in the 2010s?

Section B
1. Why do you think an early radio was called a wireless?
2. Why do you need hot water in a kitchen?

Section C
Carefully draw and colour a picture of a 1930s kitchen.

Changes in the Home 1930 - 2010

In the 1930s the main source of heating was the coal fire. Kitchen sinks only had cold water taps. Washing was done in a dolly tub. Entertainment was provided by the wireless and the wind up gramophone.

In the 1950s gas fires heated many homes and sinks now had a hot tap. The first black and white televisions began to appear. The radiogram could now play ten records automatically.

By the 1970s many homes were heated with central heating. Kitchens now had fridges. Colour televisions that could receive 4 channels became popular along with the first video recording machines. Hi-Fi systems with built in 3 band radios could play records and cassette tapes.

In the 1990s dishwashers, freezers tumble driers and microwave ovens became popular. Families regularly watched films through their video recorders. Music systems were becoming much smaller and played CDs. Computers and computer games started to become common.

In the 2010s computers connected to the Internet provide a range of different services. Large flat screen TVs on the lounge wall are connected to hundreds of channels and missed programmes can be watched on demand. People chat or text on mobile phones.

Answer these questions:

Section A
1. How were houses heated in the 1930s?
2. How were people entertained in the 1930s?
3. When did black and white televisions become popular?
4. How were homes heated in the 1970s?
5. How would you play a tape in the 1970s?
6. When did computers become common?
7. What do people use mobile phones for in the 2010s?
8. Which kitchen appliances became popular in the 1990s?

Section B
1. Why do you think an early radio was called a wireless?
2. Why do you need hot water in a kitchen?
3. How do you think the radiogram got its name?
4. How have televisions changed over the years?

Section C
Carefully draw and colour a picture of a 1930s kitchen.

Level 4 © Topical Resources. May be photocopied for classroom use only.

Changes in the Home 1930 - 2010

Homes have changed a lot in the last 80 years. In the 1930s the main source of heating was the coal fire. There was only a cold water supply to the sink so hot water would be heated up in a kettle on the gas cooker or range. Washing was done in a dolly tub and wrung dry in a mangle. Entertainment was provided by the wireless (early radio) and the wind up gramophone (early record player). Evenings could be spent singing songs around the family piano.

In the 1950s gas fires heated many homes. Electric cookers became popular and sinks now had a hot tap. An electric washer was placed next to the sink on 'wash day' and clothes fed through an electric mangle. The first televisions began to appear. They had very small screens with black and white pictures. People used large magnifying glasses to make their picture look bigger. The electric radiogram could now play ten records automatically one after the other.

By the 1970s many homes were heated with central heating. This meant you did not have to get dressed in a freezing cold bedroom on winter mornings. Kitchens now had electric ovens you could time and fridges for keeping food fresh. Ice cream could now be available daily and was no longer a rare treat! Colour televisions that could receive 4 channels became popular along with the first video recording machines. Hi-Fi systems with built in 3 band radios could play records and cassette tapes.

In the 1990s your lounge may have a coal effect gas fire as well as central heating. Double glazed windows help to keep the room warm and the traffic noise out. The kitchen has fitted units with wipe down surfaces. Dishwashers, freezers, tumble driers and microwave ovens became popular. The TV could receive 54 channels using a satellite dish. Families regularly watched films through their video recorders. Music systems were becoming much smaller and played CDs. Computers and computer games started to become common.

In the 2010s more people heat their homes efficiently with log burning stoves, solar panels and lots of insulation. Large kitchens are popular for entertaining friends. Computers connected to the Internet provide a range of different services such as Facebook. Large flat screens TVs on the lounge wall are connected to hundreds of channels and missed programmes can be watched on demand. People chat or text on mobile phones.

Answer these questions:

Section A
1. How were houses heated in the 1930s?
2. How were people entertained in the 1930s?
3. When did black and white televisions become popular?
4. How were homes heated in the 1970s?
5. How would you play a tape in the 1970s?
6. When did computers become common?
7. What do people use mobile phones for in the 2010s?
8. Which kitchen appliances became popular in the 1990s?
9. What did families use video recorders for?

Section B
1. Why do you think an early radio was called a wireless?
2. Why do you need hot water in a kitchen?
3. How do you think the radiogram got its name?
4. How have televisions changed over the years?
5. How do you think people reacted when they first saw a television set?
6. Describe getting out of bed in the winter with no central heating!
7. Why did ice cream used to be a 'rare treat'?

Section C
Carefully draw and colour a picture of a 1930s kitchen.

The Rise of 'Pop Music'

The wireless brought modern musical songs to millions of homes in the 1930s and 40s. During the war the songs of Vera Lynn, Gracie Fields and George Formby were popular. Elvis Presley appeared on the scene in the 1950s. In the 1960s The Beatles, a British group was very popular. In 1985 a TV audience of 2 billion people saw the Live Aid Concert. The music industry uses pop charts, pop magazines and the Internet to increase sales of its music.

Copy this writing and fill in the gaps:

The Rise of 'Pop Music'

The _____ brought modern musical songs to millions of homes in the 1930s and 40s. During the war the songs of _____ _____, Vera Lynn and Gracie Fields were popular. In the 1950s ____ _____ appeared on the scene. In the 1960s The Beatles, a _____ group was very popular. In 1985 a TV audience of 2 billion people saw the Live Aid _____. The pop music industry uses pop _____ and pop charts to increase sales of its records.

Level 2

© Topical Resources. May be photocopied for classroom use only.

The Rise of 'Pop Music'

'Pop music' is short for popular music. The wireless brought modern musical songs to millions of homes in the 1930s and 40s. During the war the songs of Vera Lynn, Gracie Fields and George Formby were popular.

The American 'Rock and Roll' performer Elvis Presley appeared on the scene in the 1950s. His performances were described as 'explosive'. In the 1960s British pop music was strongly influenced by The Beatles. 'Beatle-mania' was the name given to the behaviour of the hoards of fans that followed them.

Music on vinyl records was replaced by music cassettes, then by CDs and finally by music downloaded from the Internet. In 1985 technology made it possible for the Live Aid Concert to be transmitted to a television audience of 2 billion people.

The pop music industry uses charts such as the 'top 40 downloads', pop magazines, fan clubs, pop fashion and pop TV shows to increase sales of its music.

Answer these questions:

Section A
1. What is 'Pop Music' short for?
2. What brought music to millions of homes in the 1930s?
3. When did Elvis Presley appear?
4. Who influenced pop music in the 1960s?
5. Name four different ways people listened to music.
6. How many people saw the Live Aid concert on TV?
7. How does the pop industry increase sales of music?

Section B
1. What do you think is meant by an 'explosive performance'?
2. What is meant by the term 'Beatle-mania'?

Section C
Carefully draw and colour a picture of the 'The Beatles'.

The Rise of 'Pop Music'

'Pop music' is short for popular music. The wireless brought modern musical songs to millions of homes in the 1930s and 40s. During the war the songs of Vera Lynn, Gracie Fields and George Formby brought comedy and romance to many people separated by the fighting during World War II.

During the 1950s teenagers in work had money to spend. The American 'Rock and Roll' performer Elvis Presley appeared on the scene about this time. His performances were described as 'explosive' when he sang about young love. In the 1960's British pop music was strongly influenced by The Beatles. 'Beatle-mania' was the name given to the behaviour of the hoards of fans that followed them wherever they went.

Popular music has developed with the changes in technology. Music recorded on vinyl records was followed later by music cassettes. CDs brought better quality to recordings and now most popular music is downloaded from the Internet to be played on MP3 players. In 1985 technology made it possible for the Live Aid Concert to be transmitted to a television audience of 2 billion people.

The pop music industry uses pop charts such as the 'top 40 downloads', pop magazines, fan clubs, pop fashion, pop TV shows and pop 'promos' (promotional video films) to increase sales of their artists' music.

.

Answer these questions:

Section A
1 What is 'Pop Music' short for?
2 What brought music to millions of homes in the 1930s?
3 When did Elvis Presley appear?
4 Who influenced pop music in the 1960s?
5 Name four different ways people listened to music.
6 How many people saw the Live Aid concert on TV?
7 How does the pop industry increase sales of music?
8 Which artists were popular during the war?

Section B
1 What do you think is meant by an 'explosive performance'?
2 What is meant by the term 'Beatle-mania'?
3 How did teenagers having money to spend affect the music industry?
4 How did technology make the Live Aid Concert have such a large audience?

Section C
Carefully draw and colour a picture of the 'The Beatles'

The Rise of 'Pop Music'

'Pop music' is short for popular music. Modern pop music has strong, lively rhythms and simple, often catchy, tunes. Radio brought modern musical songs to millions of homes in the 1930s and 40s. Thousands flocked to buy sheet music of the latest popular tunes to play on their pianos. During the war the songs of Vera Lynn, Gracie Fields and George Formby brought comedy and romance to many people separated by the fighting during World War II.

During the 1950s teenagers in work had money to spend. They were listening to music that was different from the tastes of their parents. The American 'Rock and Roll' performer Elvis Presley appeared on the scene about this time. His performances were described as 'explosive' when he sang about young love and rebellion. His success was measured in record sales and film appearances.

In the 1960s British pop music was strongly influenced by The Beatles. The four members, John Lennon, Paul McCartney, George Harrison and Ringo Starr, all came from Liverpool. After appearances on TV's Top of the Pops' and number one singles, the name 'Beatle-mania' was given to the behaviour of the hoards of fans that followed them wherever they went. They are famous for a variety of songs such as the love ballad 'Yesterday' and the nursery rhyme style 'Yellow Submarine'.

Popular music has developed with the changes in technology. The wireless first brought popular music into the home. Music recorded on vinyl records was later followed by tapes in music cassettes. CDs brought better quality to recordings and now most popular music is downloaded from the Internet to be played on MP3 players. In 1985 technology made it possible for the Live Aid Concert to be transmitted to a television audience of 2 billion people. This was staged to draw attention to a famine in Ethiopia. It was played simultaneously to a crowd of 72,000 in London, England and 90,000 in Philadelphia, USA.

The pop music industry uses pop charts such as the 'top 40 downloads', pop magazines, fan clubs, pop fashion, pop TV shows and pop 'promos' (promotional video films) to increase sales of their artists' records. MTV is devoted solely to playing pop promos. Recent developments include huge stadium concert tours such as those played by Take That and television talent shows such as The X-Factor which gives ordinary members of the public the opportunity to sing live on Saturday night television.

Answer these questions:

Section A
1. What is 'Pop Music' short for?
2. What brought music to millions of homes in the 1930s?
3. When did Elvis Presley appear?
4. Who influenced pop music in the 1960s?
5. Name four different ways people listened to music.
6. How many people saw the Live Aid concert on TV?
7. How does the pop industry increase sales of music?
8. Which artists were popular during the war?
9. Who were the four members of 'The Beatles'?

Section B
1. What do you think is meant by an 'explosive performance'?
2. What is meant by the term 'Beatle-mania'?
3. How did teenagers having money to spend affect the music industry?
4. How did technology make the Live Aid Concert have such a large audience?
5. Why do you think 'thousands flocked to buy sheet music'?
6. Why was the 'Live Aid Concert' staged?
7. Do you think talent shows are a good way to find new performers? Give reasons for your answer.

Section C
Carefully draw and colour a picture of the 'The Beatles'

Travel by Car

One of the biggest changes in Britain since 1930 is the use of the family car. In 1930 there were 1.5 million cars on the road. The Austin 7 was only £100 and led to more cars on the road. The Morris 1000 was invented after World War II. The first motorway opened in 1958. After this, car ownership shot up from 3 million to 24 million. By the 1990s the motorways had daily traffic jams. In 2010 there were over 30 million cars on the roads in Britain. Electric cars are now becoming more and more popular.

Nissan leaf

Austin 7

Copy this writing and fill in the gaps:

Travel by Car

The use of the family _____ is one of the biggest changes in Britain since 1930. There were 1.5 _____ cars on the road in 1930. The Austin 7 was only £100 and led to more cars on the _____. After World War II the Morris 1000 was _____. In 1958 the first motorway opened. After this, car _____ shot up from 3 million to 24 million. The _____ had daily traffic jams by the 1990s.

In 2010 there were over 30 million cars on the roads in Britain. _____cars are now becoming more popular.

Travel by Car

One of the biggest changes in Britain since 1930 is the use of the family car. There were only one and a half million cars on the road. In 1923 Austin introduced the Austin 7, which could be purchased for £100. This led to more cars on the road.

After the war the Morris Minor, a small family car, available as a saloon, an estate and a convertible, was invented. Land Rover also brought out its first utility vehicle, which is still for sale today.

The first motorway, the M6, was opened in 1958. Car ownership shot up from 3 million to 24 million. The original Mini was invented. By the 1990s even the motorways were becoming scenes of daily traffic jams due to the number of people using them.

In 2010 there were over 30 million cars on the roads in Britain. Busy city traffic has led to concerns about the environment so more people are turning to electric cars. The Nissan Leaf is the first mass-produced all electric car to be built in Britain.

Nissan leaf
Austin 7

Answer these questions:

Section A
1. What is one of the biggest changes in Britain since 1930?
2. What did an Austin 7 cost?
3. When did Land Rover bring out its first car?
4. When was the first motorway opened?
5. What happened to motorways in the 1990s?
6. How many cars were on the roads in 2010?
7. What is the name of the first mass-produced electric car?

Section B
1. Why did the Austin 7 lead to more cars on the road?
2. Why do you think the motorways encouraged more use of cars?

Section C
Carefully draw and colour a picture of a car.

Travel by Car

One of the biggest changes in Britain since 1930 is the use of the family car. In 1930 there were only one and a half million cars on the road. In 1923 Herbert Austin introduced the Austin 7, which could be purchased for £100. This led to more cars on the road. More lorries carrying goods also took to the roads.

During World War II car factories were used to build tanks and other weapons. After the war the Morris Minor, a popular small family car available as a saloon, an estate and a convertible, was invented. Land Rover also brought out its first utility vehicle, a version of which is still for sale today.

The first motorway, the M6, was opened in 1958. It was a great success and many other motorways followed. Car ownership during this time shot up from 3 million to 24 million. The original Mini car was invented. By the 1990s even the motorways were becoming scenes of daily traffic jams due to the number of people using them.

In 2010 there were over 30 million cars on the roads in Britain. Busy town and city traffic has led to concerns about how traffic fumes affect the environment. The motor industry is responding to the problem by building electric city cars. The Nissan Leaf is the first mass-produced all electric car to be built in Britain.

Nissan leaf

Austin 7

Answer these questions:

Section A
1 What is one of the biggest changes in Britain since 1930?
2 What did an Austin 7 cost?
3 When did Land Rover bring out its first car?
4 When was the first motorway opened?
5 What happened to motorways in the 1990s?
6 How many cars were on the roads in 2010?
7 What is the name of the first mass-produced electric car?
8 What different types of Morris Minor were available?

Section B
1 Why did the Austin 7 lead to more cars on the road?
2 Why do you think the motorways encouraged more use of cars?
3 Why do you think cars were not built during World War II?
4 How have cars affected the environment?

Section C
Carefully draw and colour a picture of a car.

Level 4   © **Topical Resources.** May be photocopied for classroom use only.

Travel by Car

One of the biggest changes in Britain since 1930 is the use of the family car. In 1930 there were only one and a half million cars on the road. The first cars were very large and owned by wealthy families. In 1923 Herbert Austin introduced the Austin 7. This was a tiny four-seater car, which could be purchased for £100. Families who travelled by motorbike and sidecar could now hope to save up and buy a proper car.

More cars on the roads led to traffic jams especially on roads to the seaside on summer weekends. Unemployed men were given work in the 1930s making new dual carriageways to bypass towns and villages. More lorries carrying goods took to the roads as they could deliver to many more places than the railways. The lorries added to the over crowding on the roads.

During World War II, petrol was scarce and car factories were used to build tanks and other weapons. After the war many cars were made for export. This meant cars made in Britain were mainly sold in other countries around the world. About this time Morris invented the Morris 1000, a popular small family car available as a saloon, an estate and a convertible. Land Rover also brought out its first utility vehicle, a version of which is still for sale today.

The first motorway, the M6, was opened in December 1958. It bypassed Preston in Lancashire, which had serious traffic jams. It was a great success and many other motorways followed, freeing towns from traffic jams. Car ownership during this time shot up from 3 million to 24 million. The original Mini car was invented. This was another tiny family car designed by Austin, this time working with Morris. Other popular models included the Ford Anglia and the Vauxhall Viva. By the 1990s even the motorways were becoming scenes of daily traffic jams due to the number of people using them.

In 2010 there were over 30 million cars on the roads in Britain. Many women now go to work by car after dropping their children off at school. Busy town and city traffic has led to concerns about how traffic fumes affect the environment. The motor industry is responding to the problem by building electric city cars. After charging them up at home, they can travel about 100 miles the next day. The Nissan Leaf is the first mass-produced electric car to be built in Britain and the first all electric car to be awarded the 'Car of the Year Award'.

Nissan leaf

Austin 7

Answer these questions:

Section A
1. What is one of the biggest changes in Britain since 1930?
2. What did an Austin 7 cost?
3. When did Land Rover bring out its first car?
4. When was the first motorway opened?
5. What happened to motorways in the 1990s?
6. How many cars were on the roads in 2010?
7. What is the name of the first mass-produced electric car?
8. What different types of Morris Minor were available?
9. What work were unemployed men given in the 1930s?

Section B
1. Why did the Austin 7 lead to more cars on the road?
2. Why do you think the motorways encouraged more use of cars?
3. Why do you think cars were not built during World War II?
4. How have cars affected the environment?
5. Why were traffic jams on roads to the seaside worse on sunny days?
6. What do you understand by the word 'export'?
7. How would more working mothers affect the number of cars on the road?

Section C
Carefully draw and colour a picture of a car.

Passenger Aircraft and Holidays Abroad

In the 1930s the British inventor Frank Whittle and a German inventor, Hans von Ohain, tried to make a jet engine power a plane. Ohain's engine flew first. Their work made way for the first jet airliner called The Comet. This first flew in 1949.

The passenger jet altered the way a lot of people in Britain took their holidays. People could now afford to fly off for two weeks holiday in the sun. Disney Land in Florida has become a particularly popular place to visit for families with young children.

The Comet - the first jet powered passenger plane.

Copy this writing and fill in the gaps:

Passenger Aircraft and Holidays Abroad

In the 1930s the British inventor Frank _____ and a German inventor, Hans von _____, tried to make a plane powered by a jet engine. _____ engine flew first. Their work made way for the first jet airliner called The _____. This first flew in 1949. The passenger jet altered the way a lot of people in Britain took their _____. People could now afford to fly off for two weeks holiday in the _____. Disney World in _____ has become a popular place to visit for families with young children.

Level 2   © **Topical Resources.** May be photocopied for classroom use only.

Passenger Aircraft and Holidays Abroad

In the 1930s the British inventor Frank Whittle and a German designer, Hans von Ohain, tried to make a jet engine power a plane. Ohain's engine flew first. World War II broke out the next month.

The German Messerschmitt Me 262 was the world's first operational jet fighter aircraft. The Gloster Meteor was the first British jet fighter. Their designs paved the way for the first jet airliner, The Comet. This first flew in 1949 and was very fast.

The passenger jet altered the way a lot of people in Britain took their holidays. People could afford to fly off for two weeks holiday in the sun. Disney World in Florida has become a particularly popular destination for families with young children.

Many British people returned home from their holidays having tried local food. As a result Britain has developed an appetite for foreign meals and many Indian, Chinese, Italian and other restaurants have appeared throughout the country.

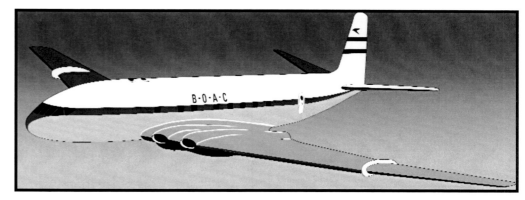

The Comet - the first jet powered passenger plane.

Answer these questions:

Section A
1. Which British inventor worked on a jet engine?
2. Which German inventor worked on a jet engine?
3. Whose engine flew first?
4. What was the first jet airliner called?
5. How did people get to their holidays in the sun?
6. Which holiday is popular for families with children?
7. What did British people try on holiday?

Section B
1. How did the jet airliner affect where people could go on holiday?
2. Why have many foreign restaurants opened in Britain?

Section C
Carefully draw and colour a picture of 'The Comet'.

Passenger Aircraft and Holidays Abroad

In the 1930s two men tried to make a jet engine to power an aeroplane. The British inventor Frank Whittle recorded his ideas in 1930. A German designer, Hans von Ohain, started work later. His engine first flew in August 1939. War broke out between Germany and Britain the next month.

The German Messerschmitt Me 262 was the world's first operational jet fighter aircraft. The Gloster Meteor was the first British jet fighter and went into service shortly afterwards. Their designs paved the way for the first jet airliner, The Comet. It first flew in 1949 and could fly twice as fast as previous passenger planes. It was also quieter and much more comfortable to travel in.

The passenger jet altered the way a lot of people in Britain took their holidays. For the first time they could afford to fly off to Spain or Greece for two weeks holiday in the sun. Package holidays included a hotel by the beach and all meals provided. Later, holidays as far away as America and Africa were on offer. Disney Land in Florida is a particularly popular destination for families with young children.

Many British people returned home having sampled local food. As a result Britain has developed an appetite for foreign meals and many Indian, Chinese, Italian and other restaurants have appeared throughout the country.

The Comet - the first jet powered passenger plane.

Answer these questions:

Section A
1. Which British inventor worked on a jet engine?
2. Which German inventor worked on a jet engine?
3. Whose engine flew first?
4. What was the first jet airliner called?
5. How did people get to their holidays in the sun?
6. Which holiday is popular for families with children?
7. What did British people try on holiday?
8. What was the world's first jet fighter aircraft called?

Section B
1. How did the jet airliner affect where people could go on holiday?
2. Why have many foreign restaurants opened in Britain?
3. What does the phrase 'paved the way' mean?
4. Why do you think many families like to visit Disney World in Florida?

Section C
Carefully draw and colour a picture of 'The Comet'.

Passenger Aircraft and Holidays Abroad

A jet engine produces a high-speed stream of hot gases to push an aircraft through the air. A Greek mathematician named Hero first explored the idea in the first century AD. He made a metal ball containing boiling water spin as the steam escaped out of two small holes.

In the 1930s two men independently tried to make a jet engine to power an aeroplane. The British inventor Frank Whittle recorded his ideas in 1930, but his first engine did not fly until 1941. A German designer, Hans von Ohain, started work a little later, but he received immediate financial help for his design, and his engine first flew in August 1939. War broke out between Germany and Britain the next month.

The German Messerschmitt Me 262 was the world's first operational jet fighter aircraft. It went into service just before the end of the Second World War. The Gloster Meteor was the first British jet fighter and went into service shortly afterwards. Both planes were too late to have any real effect on the war but their designs paved the way for the first commercial jet airliner, The Comet. It first flew in 1949 and could fly twice as fast as previous passenger planes. It was also quieter and much more comfortable to travel in.

The invention of the passenger jet plane altered the way a lot of people in Britain took their holidays. For the first time they could afford to escape the unpredictable British weather and fly to the Greek Islands or the Algarve in Portugal for two weeks holiday in the sun. Package holidays included a hotel by the beach and all meals provided. As passenger jets improved and people became more well off, holidays as far away as America and Africa were on offer. People now regularly fly to destinations all over the world. Disney Land in Florida is a particularly popular destination for families with young children.

Many British holiday makers returned home having sampled the delights of local food. As a result of this, Britain has developed an appetite for foreign and exotic meals and many Indian, Chinese, Italian and other restaurants have appeared throughout the country. Another consequence of jet travel is fewer people spend their holidays in traditional seaside resorts such as Blackpool or Torquay.

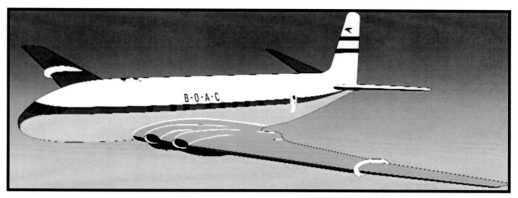

The Comet - the first jet powered passenger plane.

Answer these questions:

Section A
1. Which British inventor worked on a jet engine?
2. Which German inventor worked on a jet engine?
3. Whose engine flew first?
4. What was the first jet airliner called?
5. How did people get to their holidays in the sun?
6. Which holiday is popular for families with children?
7. What did British people try on holiday?
8. What was the world's first jet fighter aircraft called?
9. Who was the first person to try a simple jet engine?

Section B
1. How did the jet airliner affect where people could go on holiday?
2. Why have many foreign restaurants opened in Britain?
3. What does the phrase 'paved the way' mean?
4. Why do you think many families like to visit Disney World in Florida?
5. What do you think the first passengers thought of The Comet?
6. Why did the first jet fighters have little effect on World War II?
7. Why do you think Ohain's jet flew before Whittle's jet?

Section C
Carefully draw and colour a picture of 'The Comet'.

Early Space Travel

In 1961 the Russian, Yuri Gagarin, was the first man in space. In 1965, another Russian made the first space walk. In 1967 the Americans launched the largest and most powerful rocket ever used. The first moon landing took place in 1969. Apollo 11 was put into orbit around the Moon. Neil Armstrong and Buzz Aldrin flew down to the Moon in the Lunar Module. Millions of people in Britain stopped what they were doing and watched. Neil Armstrong said, "That's one small step for a man, one giant leap for mankind."

Copy this writing and fill in the gaps:

Early Space Travel

The first man in space was the Russian, Yuri _____, in 1961. Another Russian made the first ____ walk in 1965. The _____ launched the largest rocket ever used in 1967. The first moon landing took place in _____. Apollo 11 was put into orbit around the Moon. Neil _____ and Buzz Aldrin flew down to the Moon in the ____ Module. In Britain, millions of people stopped what they were doing and _____. Neil Armstrong said, "That's one small step for a man, one _____ leap for mankind."

Early Space Travel

In 1961 the Russians used Vostock 1 to make Yuri Gagarin the first man in space. In 1965, another Russian, Alexei Leonar, made the first space walk.

In 1967 the Americans launched their Saturn V rocket. This was the largest and most powerful rocket ever used.

The first moon landing took place in 1969. Apollo 11 was put into orbit around the Moon. Neil Armstrong and Buzz Aldrin flew down to the Moon in the Lunar Module. Millions of people in Britain stopped what they were doing and watched. Neil Armstrong said, "That's one small step for a man, one giant leap for mankind."

The Space Shuttle replaced Apollo. The Shuttle was used to place satellites for mobile phones and the International Space Station into orbit. The British businessman, Richard Branson, is hoping to be the first to offer space flights for paying passengers.

Answer these questions:

Section A
1. Who was the first man in space?
2. Who made the first space walk?
3. What was special about Saturn V?
4. When did the first moon landing take place?
5. What did millions of British people do when the first step was made?
6. What was the Space Shuttle used for?
7. Who hopes to offer space flights for paying passengers?

Section B
1. How do you think people watching the first step on the Moon felt at the time?
2. How do you think Neil Armstrong felt as he made the first step on the Moon?

Section C
Carefully draw and colour a picture of a man on the Moon.

Early Space Travel

In 1961 the Russians used Vostock 1 to make Yuri Gagarin the first man in space. In 1964 Voskhod 1 took three Russian cosmonauts into space. In 1965, another Russian, Alexei Leonar, made the first space walk. At this point Russia seemed to be winning the space race.

In 1967 the Americans launched their Saturn V rocket for the first time. This was the largest and most powerful rocket ever used and was designed to take the first men to the Moon. In 1968 Apollo 8 made the first manned flight to the Moon, orbiting ten times before returning to the Earth.

The first moon landing took place in 1969. Apollo 11 was put into orbit around the Moon. Neil Armstrong and Buzz Aldrin flew down to the Moon in the Lunar Module. Millions of people in Britain stopped what they were doing and watched the first step on the Moon. Neil Armstrong said, "That's one small step for a man, one giant leap for mankind."

Five more moon landings were made but the costs were huge. The Space Shuttle replaced Apollo because it could be used again. The Shuttle was used to place satellites for mobile phones and the International Space Station into orbit. The British businessman, Richard Branson, is hoping to be the first to offer regular space flights for paying passengers using the Virgin Galactic spacecraft.

Answer these questions:

Section A
1. Who was the first man in space?
2. Who made the first space walk?
3. What was special about Saturn V?
4. When did the first moon landing take place?
5. What did millions of British people do when the first step was made?
6. What was the Space Shuttle used for?
7. Who hopes to offer space flights for paying passengers?
8. How many Moon landings were made?

Section B
1. How do you think people watching the first step on the Moon felt at the time?
2. How do you think Neil Armstrong felt as he made the first step on the Moon?
3. What is meant by the term 'the space race'?
4. Why do you think Armstrong said, "That's one small step for a man, one giant leap for mankind."

Section C
Carefully draw and colour a picture of a man on the Moon.

Early Space Travel

During World War II, the Germans developed the first working rockets and used these to bomb London. After the war the Russians were the first to use a rocket to send a satellite called Sputnick 1 into orbit around the Earth. This was followed by the much bigger Sputnick 2, carrying a dog called Laika. Shortly after, the Americans launched their first satellite. The 'Space Race' had begun and the British people watched with great interest.

In 1959 the Russians sent an unmanned space probe around the Moon sending back the first ever photographs of the far side of the Moon. In 1961 the Russians used Vostock 1 to make Yuri Gagarin the first man in space. In 1964 Voskhod 1 took three Russian cosmonauts into space. In 1965, another Russian, Alexei Leonar, made the first space walk. At this point Russia seemed to be winning the space race because it had large rockets which carried heavy loads.

In 1967 the Americans launched their Saturn V rocket for the first time. This was the largest and most powerful rocket ever used and was designed to take the first men to the Moon. In 1968 Apollo 8 made the first manned flight to the Moon, orbiting ten times before returning to the Earth.

The first moon landing took place on 20th July 1969. Apollo 11, after being launched by the giant Saturn V rocket, was put into orbit around the Moon. Mike Collins stayed in the Command Module while Neil Armstrong and Buzz Aldrin flew down to the Moon in the Lunar Module. They landed in a place known as the Sea of Tranquillity. Millions of people in Britain and other parts of the world stopped what they were doing and watched the first step on the Moon. Neil Armstrong said, "That's one small step for a man, one giant leap for mankind."

Five more Moon landings were made but the costs were huge. The Space Shuttle replaced the Apollo Spacecraft. This made a lot more financial sense as the Shuttle could land like an aircraft and be used again. The Shuttle flew from 1981 to 2011 carrying crews of 7 and different cargoes into space. The Shuttle has been used to place satellites for use by TV signals, mobile phones and 'Sat Nav' devices into orbit. It has also carried many sections of the International Space Station, the single biggest man-made satellite in orbit. The British businessman, Richard Branson, is hoping to be the first to offer regular space flights for paying passengers using the Virgin Galactic spacecraft.

Answer these questions:

Section A
1. Who was the first man in space?
2. Who made the first space walk?
3. What was special about Saturn V?
4. When did the first moon landing take place?
5. What did millions of British people do when the first step was made?
6. What was the Space Shuttle used for?
7. Who hopes to offer space flights for paying passengers?
8. How many moon landings were made?
9. Who developed the first working rockets?

Section B
1. How do you think people watching the first step on the Moon felt at the time?
2. How do you think Neil Armstrong felt as he made the first step on the Moon?
3. What is meant by the term 'the space race'?
4. Why do you think Armstrong said, "That's one small step for a man, one giant leap for mankind."
5. Why was the Space Shuttle less expensive to run?
6. Why do you think the space race was 'watched with great interest'?
7. How would you feel about taking a flight into space?

Section C
Carefully draw and colour a picture of a man on the Moon.

The Computer Age Begins

In 1943 the first electronic computer was built in Britain. It was called Colossus and was used to crack enemy codes during World War II. Since then, computers have become smaller and cheaper to buy. The first home computers went on sale in the 1980s. They could be used for working and playing games. Nowadays most homes have a computer with access to the Internet. People keep in touch through Facebook, TV can be watched and shopping can be ordered. The home computer is changing the way people live their lives.

Copy this writing and fill in the gaps:

The Computer Age Begins

The first _____ computer was built in Britain in 1943. It was used to crack enemy codes during World War II and it was called ____. Since then, computers have become smaller and cheaper to buy. In the _____ the first home computers went on sale. They could be used for working and playing _____. Nowadays most homes have a computer with access to the _____. People keep in touch through Facebook, _____ can be ordered and ____ can be watched. The home computer is _____ the way people live their lives.

The Computer Age Begins

In 1943 the first electronic computer was built in Britain. It was called Colossus and was used to crack enemy codes during World War II. It was powered by glass valves.

In the 1950s transistors replaced valves. In the 1960s integrated circuits were used. In the 1970s microchips were used. All of these developments made computers smaller and cheaper to buy.

The first home computers went on sale in the 1980s. They could be used for word processing, keeping databases, spreadsheets and games.

Nowadays most homes have a computer with access to the Internet. Messages are sent instantly by email. People keep in touch with their friends through Facebook. You Tube can be used to watch homemade videos. Missed TV programmes can be watched. Shopping can be ordered and delivered to your door. The home computer is rapidly changing the way people live their lives.

Answer these questions:

Section A
1. Where was the first electronic computer built?
2. What was this computer used for?
3. What replaced valves?
4. What powered computers in the 1970s?
5. When did the first home computers go on sale?
6. What do most home computers have access to?
7. How can instant messages be sent?

Section B
1. How did computers change from the 1940s to the 1970s?
2. What sort of things do you use a computer for

Section C
Carefully draw and colour a picture of Colossus.

The Computer Age Begins

In 1943 the first electronic computer was built in Britain. It was called Colossus and was used to crack enemy codes during World War II. This was an enormous machine powered by electronic glass valves, which were unreliable.

In the 1950s transistors, small electronic components, replaced valves. In the 1960s integrated circuits were used. In the 1970s microchips were used. All of these developments made computers smaller, more reliable, more powerful and much cheaper to buy. The first home computers went on sale in the 1980s.

The Sinclair ZX Spectrum was one of the first full colour home computers. It could be used for word processing, keeping databases, spreadsheets and games. This machine became so popular that many companies were set up to create programs and games for it.

Nowadays most homes have a simple to use, powerful computer with access to the Internet. Messages are sent instantly by email. People keep in touch with their friends through Facebook. You Tube can be used to watch homemade videos. Missed TV programmes can be watched. Shopping can be ordered and delivered to your door. The home computer is rapidly changing the way people live their lives.

Answer these questions:

Section A
1. Where was the first electronic computer built?
2. What was this computer used for?
3. What replaced valves?
4. What powered computers in the 1970s?
5. When did the first home computers go on sale?
6. What do most home computers have access to?
7. How can instant messages be sent?
8. How can people keep in touch with friends?

Section B
1. How did computers change from the 1940s to the 1970s?
2. What sort of things do you use a computer for?
3. How can you tell the ZX Spectrum was very popular?
4. Name one way computers have changed the way people live.

Section C
Carefully draw and colour a picture of Colossus.